CONTEMPORARY MUSICIANS
AND THEIR MUSIC™

Justin Timberlake

Holly Cefrey

ROSEN PUBLISHING

New York

To the talents of tomorrow, Meilleurs Voeux!

Published in 2009 by The Rosen Publishing Group, Inc.
29 East 21st Street, New York, NY 10010

Copyright © 2009 by The Rosen Publishing Group, Inc.

First Edition

Library of Congress Cataloging-in-Publication Data

Cefrey, Holly.
Justin Timberlake / Holly Cefrey.
     p. cm.—(Contemporary musicians and their music)
Includes bibliographical references.
ISBN-13: 978-1-4042-1815-4 (library binding)
ISBN-13: 978-1-4358-5123-8 (pbk)
ISBN-13: 978-1-4042-7868-4 (6 pack)
1. Timberlake, Justin, 1981– —Juvenile literature. 2. Singers—United States—Biography—Juvenile literature. I. Title.
ML3930.T58 C44
782.42164092—dc22
[B]
                                                                                    2007051807

Manufactured in Malaysia

On the cover: A photograph of Justin Timberlake.

Contents

Introduction

In the entertainment industry, some multitalented artists are known as triple threats. A triple threat is an artist who has the not-too-common ability to expertly showcase different talents. Usually, this kind of artist can act, sing, and dance—all equally well. Depending on the industry area, triple threats can also include artists who can produce, write, compose, and direct, in addition to the original three skill sets.

Artists and actors submit resumes—just like a career resume—to talent and casting agents in order to be considered for parts in movies, television shows and commercials, theater productions, and

Justin Timberlake is a globally recognized musical talent. Here, he performs in Abu Dhabi, United Arab Emirates, in 2007.

other creative projects. These resumes provide information about an artist's prior experiences, training, and special skills. When a casting agent reads on a resume that an artist is a triple threat, he or she puts that artist into a special category that gets greater consideration for diverse and challenging roles. This is because the more developed you are across different areas of talent, the more versatile and successful you are as an artist.

An area of entertainment that especially relies upon triple threat skills is music. Today's videos and multimedia projects require that musicians—even if they have no interest in acting—be able to show emotion to fans and other viewers. Musical artists need to perform in support of the story that their video is telling. They must be convincing in this "mini-musical" movie that is the modern music video.

The world's most successful recording artists are those who showcase their triple threat skills in videos and multimedia projects. They emerge as not just singers but as artists who surprise us in other ways and make us want to see more. Justin Timberlake is one of today's most engaging triple threats within the entertainment industry. Although Timberlake is still early in his solo career, the sky seems to be his limit.

Chapter One

Justin Randall Timberlake of Tennessee

Justin Randall Timberlake was born on Saturday, January 31, 1981, in Memphis, Tennessee. Memphis has continuously added to the global entertainment industry for more than one hundred years. The musical categories, or genres, of blues, jazz, gospel, and rock and roll can be traced to the city of Memphis. Among its brightest stars are Johnny Cash, B. B. King, and Elvis Presley. According to *Spin* magazine, Memphis is the "home of the blues, birthplace of rock, and the capitol of soul."

Timberlake grew up in a suburb called Millington, which is just 12 miles (19.3 kilometers) from downtown Memphis. It is a twenty-minute drive from Millington to Elvis Presley's estate of Graceland and the world-famous Beale Street, which is called "the home of the blues." The natural scenery of Millington,

A main factor in Memphis's musical history is Beale Street. Musical careers have been launched in the many clubs and bars of the street, which offer the best of the blues.

Tennessee, includes vast peach orchards, cotton fields, woods, and lakes.

Early Signs of Talent

Religion and music were very prominent in Justin Timberlake's background. One of his grandfathers was a Baptist minister. His mother, Lynn Bomar (now remarried as Lynn Harless), and his father, Randall (Randy) Timberlake, married in 1979. Lynn told *Rolling Stone* magazine in 2006 that Justin's musical abilities came from his father's side. Randall sang and played bass in a bluegrass band with Lynn's brother. Randall was also the choir director at the local Baptist church.

Justin showed musical ability at an early age. Lynn told *Rolling Stone* that when her son was about four months old, she would place him in his car seat, atop the kitchen counter. She and Randall would play music and "he'd kick his legs to the beat. We'd change the music, and he'd kick his legs to the new beat." At the age of two, Justin was "adding harmony to the songs on the radio," beamed his mother to *Rolling Stone*.

Justin attended E. E. Jeter Elementary School, where he was a spelling bee champion and a basketball player, as reported by Shelby County's *Staffer* magazine. He didn't attend a regular high school. It became evident that Justin was meant to perform, which meant that a regular school wouldn't do. He was educated through private tutors and independent study programs of the University of Nebraska (Lincoln), according to MTV. He received his high school diploma in May 2000 at the age of nineteen in front of twenty thousand of his Memphis fans. Earlier on his graduation day, he visited his old elementary school and announced that he would give money to fund a music program for the school.

Star Search

At age eleven, Justin Timberlake appeared as a contestant on *Star Search*, hosted by Ed McMahon. The televised competition featured talented (and sometimes not-so-talented) performers. A

The Land of Talent: Tennessee

The state of Tennessee has a deep, rich musical history. In 1998, the U.S. Congress recognized Bristol, Tennessee, as the true birthplace of country music. Many Scottish immigrants settled in Bristol during the 1700s. They brought old-world songs with them. These songs began to include other influences that were Irish and African. This blend of music was first known as rural mountain music. A talent agent named Ralph Peer recorded this rural mountain music for the first time in the 1920s. Peer's recordings are known as the "Bristol Sessions." They are credited as the earliest form of country music.

Nashville, Tennessee, is home to the famous Grand Ole Opry. The Grand Ole Opry is a seventy-five-year-old institution that showcases country-and-western musical talent. Artists dream of appearing at the "Opry." Many careers have been launched from within its walls, such as that of Stonewall Jackson in the late 1950s. More recently, Carrie Underwood performed Tammy Wynette's "Stand By Your Man" there to wild applause. According to *International Who's Who in Popular Music 2002*, Justin Timberlake made a guest appearance at the Opry in 1991, when he was just ten years old.

Memphis is yet another musical city in the state of Tennessee. The Library of Congress traced the roots of America's musical genres to Memphis, where blues, jazz, gospel, and rock and roll arose in the 1900s. Many innovators lived there, including Johnny Cash, Elvis Presley, W. C. Handy, Alberta Hunter, and B. B. King. Artists in Memphis experimented with ideas so that many new styles were created.

panel of five judges awarded up to four stars to these performers. Those who were awarded the most stars proceeded to the next show to compete for two more rounds. Once he or she made it past three rounds, the winning contestant went on to a championship show where the audience acted as the judges.

Justin performed as "Justin Timberlake Randall" while dressed in country-and-western garb that included a cowboy hat and fancy belt buckle. He sang "Love's Got a Hold on You" by Alan Jackson. He received three and a quarter stars from the judges. However, his competitor was awarded four stars. Even though he lost, Justin was still a good sport. He shook the winner's hand and left the stage smiling. Within a year, the young performer would join a show that would go on to produce massive star power.

With video forums like YouTube, you can see major stars in their early years. Here, a young Justin Timberlake performs on *Star Search* with the ease of a seasoned performer.

This early public performance on *Star Search* revealed Justin's interest in country music. He also idolized Michael Jackson, the King of Pop. Pop is music that is an upbeat, repetitive, and softer version of rock and roll that tends to appeal to younger audiences. As the King of Pop, Jackson was an idol to many. Justin was inspired enough to challenge himself to master Jackson's pop melodies and flashy dance moves.

A Mouseketeer

The Mickey Mouse Club was a daily television show that was produced by Walt Disney the company and Walt Disney the man. It had its debut during the early years of television, making it one of the first youth-oriented variety shows. The hour-long program originally hit the air in 1955 and ran in various versions in the following four decades.

Young triple threats, as well as everyday boys and girls without acting experience, were hired as cast members for *The Mickey Mouse Club*. These cast members were called Mouseketeers. All Mouseketeers wore black caps that were topped by two large mouse ears. The program included newsreels, "mousekartoons," singing and dancing by the cast, and special performances by guest artists. Throughout the week, *The Mickey Mouse Club* highlighted a different career so that viewers at home could get ideas about their future job plans. One of the original cast members was Annette Funicello. She went on to become a major star in musical comedies.

In the 1990s, *The Mickey Mouse Club* was reintroduced as *The All New Mickey Mouse Club*, or *MMC*. Some of today's top performers began as cast members on *The All New Mickey Mouse Club*, including Britney Spears, Christina Aguilera, Keri Russell, Ryan Gosling, and JC Chasez. Justin Timberlake joined the cast in 1993, for Seasons 6 and 7. According to *USA Today*, he felt like he found a place where he finally belonged. He said that when he landed a role on the program, he "finally fit in. There were other kids who loved to perform, and I didn't feel like an outsider."

The show offered some kind of developmental magic: many of its cast members achieved big-time success in a surprisingly short time span. New York's *Daily News* newspaper called *MMC* one of the most "celeb-making shows in television history." While the young cast members had some show business experience before joining *The All New Mickey Mouse Club*, the atmosphere at the show helped them to develop their talents even further. In 1999, during her "Genie in a Bottle" fame, Aguilera told the BBC (British Broadcasting Corporation) that *MMC* was a great training

Count the stars in this "class" photo. Many cast members of *The All New Mickey Mouse Club* have gone on to entertain the world.

ground to sharpen their talent and gain additional skills. "We got to sing and act on a regular basis with other talented people," Aguilera said. "That made us all better."

The All New Mickey Mouse Club was an ideal training ground because Aguilera, Chasez, Spears, Russell, and Gosling have all gone on to successful careers. Gosling was nominated for an Academy Award in 2007—without having any formal acting training. Justin Timberlake is no exception. He has experienced a meteoric rise as well.

Chapter Two

Syncing with the World

Justin Timberlake's world had changed tremendously by the time *The All New Mickey Mouse Club* ended in 1995. His parents divorced in 1985, when he was four years old, and they had already moved on to separate lives. Lynn married Paul Harless, a banker, in 1986. Justin's father, Randy, married a woman named Lisa. He had two children with her: Jonathan was born in 1993, and Stephen came along five years later, in 1998. In addition to two half-brothers, Justin had a half-sister. Sadly, she died shortly after childbirth in 1997.

Lynn became her son's manager. She made sure that he received the proper tutoring and training. According to *International Who's Who in Popular Music 2002*, Justin's musical training began at age eight. By the time he left *The All New*

Mixing family with business is a tricky combination. Justin and his mother, Lynn, have remained as close as can be, with a successful and strong family and professional relationship.

Mickey Mouse Club, he had gained an ample amount of stage and live performance experience, including choreographed dancing. He had also learned spokesperson skills by introducing topics on camera.

One *MMC* segment followed Justin back to Memphis, Tennessee, where he showed viewers Graceland, Elvis Presley's famous estate. He did an impersonation of Elvis. He also talked about his favorite activities, including all-terrain vehicle driving, basketball, and golf. Justin hammed it up and showed a natural ease in front of the camera.

Boy Band Magic

While on the *MMC*, Justin formed a strong friendship with JC Chasez, whose full name is Joshua Scott Chasez. The two sang and performed well together. At the same time, Christopher Alan Kirkpatrick and Joey Fatone were performing for Universal Studios in Orlando, Florida. Fatone met Chasez through a *MMC* cast member. Chasez also became friends with Kirkpatrick. Soon, all of their paths would cross in a way that would change their lives forever.

Louis (Lou) J. Pearlman owned an aviation business that provided chartered planes to famous bands for their tours. Pearlman became intrigued by the success of the group New Kids on the Block. Topping the pop music charts in the late 1980s and early 1990s, New Kids on the Block were five teenage boys whose looks and talent earned them a massive following of female fans. They happened to be one of Pearlman's clients. He

Lou Pearlman was a successful aviation business leader who turned his talents to music. He based 'N Sync and other bands on the success of New Kids on the Block.

began using his resources to create a band that would capitalize on the success of New Kids on the Block.

In 1992, Pearlman started Trans Continental Records and held auditions for talented boys. He finally hired five who fit his formula: a baby-faced one, a sensitive one, a bad boy, a heartthrob, and a jokester. According to CBS News, Pearlman spent more than $1 million over two years on training and molding the five boys into a group that would become known as the Backstreet Boys. By 1996, the Backstreet Boys were already a hit in Europe and their popularity was growing by leaps and bounds in the United States.

O-Town

Pearlman was immediately interested in repeating the success he had achieved with the Backstreet Boys. According to CBS News, he received some important advice from Smokey Robinson, a Motown artist. Based in Detroit, Michigan, Motown produced a parade of polished African American artists who dominated the pop and R & B charts in the 1960s and 1970s. Robinson advised Pearlman that he should open a Motown-like business that would focus on Caucasian artists. The new business would be called O-Town, after Orlando, Florida. As reported by

Time magazine, O-Town would be a sprawling recording and training complex where Pearlman and his team would develop a number of groups.

By 1995, Pearlman was ready to put together his next group. He already knew Chris Kirkpatrick, who had auditioned for the Backstreet Boys but did not make the cut. Conveniently, Justin Timberlake and JC Chasez had decided to continue pursuing their musical careers in Orlando during that time. Kirkpatrick spoke to them about creating a band. The group ran into Joey Fatone. They invited him to join. Fatone invited his friend Jason Watkins to join.

The group began working together with the goal of being the next top boy band. Watkins dropped out of the group before they officially signed with

Five talents came together under Lou Pearlman's leadership to form 'N Sync. Their faces and songs would be known globally in just a few short years.

King of Boy Bands . . . and Trouble

Just as 'N Sync's career began to soar, the Backstreet Boys' relationship with Lou Pearlman began to sour. They sued Pearlman in 1998 because they felt that he was making too much money without sharing enough of it. According to VH1, the Backstreet Boys received only $300,000 from a European summer tour that made $10 million. Another concern was that 'N Sync was too similar to their band. They wanted a new manager who wouldn't be representing their competitor.

The Backstreet Boys and their former manager settled out of court, but Pearlman's legal battles were only starting. Zomba, the parent company of the band's Jive Records label, sued Pearlman's Trans Continental Records. The suit was over merchandising, royalties, and control issues concerning the Backstreet Boys.

More legal troubles arose when 'N Sync threatened to record with Jive instead of RCA, which is owned by BMG. As a result, Pearlman and BMG filed a lawsuit against 'N Sync in 1999. The band filed their own suit against Pearlman, claiming that, like the Backstreet Boys, they were cheated out of millions of dollars. 'N Sync settled with Pearlman without going to court, but they no longer wanted him to manage them. They went on to record with Jive.

Pearlman's financial and legal issues did not end there. According to the Associated Press, he allegedly swindled more than $300 million from hundreds of investors. He fled the country in January 2007 to hide from the FBI. However, he was captured in Bali on June 14, 2007.

Pearlman. Timberlake's vocal coach recommended Lance Bass to fill the spot that was left empty by Watkins. Bass auditioned for Pearlman and the other members. They all liked him immediately. The group signed with Pearlman and moved to a house that he set up for them near the recording studio.

'N Sync

Justin's mom, Lynn, is credited with naming the band 'N Sync because she felt that they were "in sync." To be "in synch" means to be in harmony or agreement. The band's name also corresponds to the last letter in each member's first name—except Lance Bass, whose nickname became Lansten. The abbreviation worked with Jason Watkins's name before Lance Bass joined.

Pearlman hired studio musicians, producers, and songwriters to train the new group at O-Town, which, according to CBS News, was like a boot camp and a charm school. Talents were given vocal coaching, public relations training, image styling, and dance lessons. Public relations training was intended to make them seem polished when talking to the press and general public. Image styling would teach them how they should look and act while in the public eye. Johnny Wright, who once managed New Kids on the Block, came on board to assist the new group as well.

Some managers are "image makers." They play a big part in making the talent you see into stars. Johnny Wright shaped the star power of 'N Sync.

'N Sync released "I Want You Back" in 1996. The pop single became a top 10 hit in Germany. Their next single, "Tearin' Up My Heart," was released in 1997 in Europe, where the band immediately started to tour. The two songs were off their European-issue debut album, *NSYNC.

RCA Records offered Pearlman and his band a recording contract in 1998. RCA made the group rerecord a few songs on the album for release in the United States. *NSYNC was released stateside in May 1998. The band performed in the 1998 Summer Disney Concert. Almost right after the concert, 'N Sync's popularity soared. Everyone wanted to learn more about Pearlman's newest boy band.

The U.S. release of "I Want You Back" reached number 13 on Billboard's Hot 100 music chart. According to BMI (Broadcast

Music Incorporated), the band's debut album sold more than seven million copies. In November 1998, 'N Sync released their *Home for Christmas* album. It ultimately sold more than two million copies. The band was quickly establishing itself as a pop-hit maker. They even obtained some appearances as the opening act for Janet Jackson's Velvet Rope Tour.

Their Own Fame

'N Sync released their second pop album, *No Strings Attached*, in March 2000. It sold 1.1 million copies on the first day, reported *Wired* magazine. This made it the fastest-selling album of all time. According to BMI Music World, more than 2.42 million copies were bought within the first week. The single "Bye Bye Bye" reached the top 5 of Billboard's Hot 100. "It's Gonna Be Me," the second single from the album, reached the number-one spot. The tour to support *No Strings Attached* met with equal success, selling out nearly all of the stadiums.

In 2001, the band released *Celebrity*, its third U.S. album. *Celebrity* marked a new stage for the individual members of the band as well as the band's style. Timberlake and Chasez wrote and produced several of the tracks on the album, which reflected the band's rap influences. Rap is a musical genre that was started

The star-making of 'N Sync included dynamic, expensively produced live shows. The group sang and danced, and visuals such as these were used for effect.

in the 1970s, mainly by inner-city African American youth. This style of music has a driving beat and lyrics that are usually rapped, or spoken, instead of sung. 'N Sync's use of rap on *Celebrity* signaled the new directions that the band was exploring.

Chapter Three

Justin Timberlake the Solo Artist

His songwriting, producing, and singing contributions to the *Celebrity* album proved that Justin Timberlake had what it would take to further boost the success of 'N Sync. He told *Rolling Stone* that he was excited about the band's new direction away from straight pop music. "I did a ballad that is totally R & B," he told the magazine. "It sounds like R. Kelly could have sung it."

One of the album's producers was Rodney Jerkins. Jerkins had produced such top-selling R & B and pop acts as Whitney Houston, Mary J. Blige, and Michael Jackson. As a producer, Jerkins organizes and supervises the making of a song or entire album. Depending on how flexible the artist is, he can even write lyrics or new melodies while working on a song. Another of the album's producers was the production team the Neptunes.

The Neptunes (Pharrell Williams and Chad Hugo) worked with rap stars Nelly and Mystikal. Nelly and R & B singer Brian McKnight contributed their talents to 'N Sync's album as well.

Sliding Out of the Group

Timberlake has writing credits for seven of the thirteen songs on *Celebrity*. Some of these seven songs, including "Girlfriend" and "Gone," entered Billboard's Hot R&B/Hot Hip-Hop Singles and Tracks chart. "Gone" reached number 14. "Girlfriend," which featured Nelly, peaked at number 23 and stayed on the chart for twenty weeks.

At the 2001 MTV Awards, 'N Sync received four awards. During their performance of "Pop," Michael Jackson shared the stage with them. 'N Sync's smooth crossover into the R & B/rap arena was seen as a huge success for the boy band. A wider variety of people began to notice and accept 'N Sync, and the spotlight started to shine on individual members of the group.

In November 2001, Elton John contacted Justin Timberlake. The flamboyant pop superstar asked Timberlake if he would star in his video for "This Train Don't Stop There Anymore." Timberlake accepted, playing John's younger self in the music video. Venturing out even further on his own, Timberlake sang

Unlike bands that toil for years before being recognized, the musical community opened its arms to 'N Sync. MTV was among many organizations that recognized 'N Sync with awards.

on other artists' songs, including Brian McKnight's "My Kind of Girl" and Britney Spears's "What It's Like to Be Me." He happened to be dating Spears at the time, and her solo career was strong.

Timberlake and Spears were favorite targets for the paparazzi, photographers who seek out celebrities. The two were successful, young, attractive, and in love—all of which fascinated the public. Timberlake told *GQ* magazine in 2006 that his romantic feelings for Spears first arose during the pair's *MMC* days. "I fell in love with her from the start," he admitted. "I was infatuated with her from the moment I saw her." Shortly after this interview, the press stopped referring to him as "'N Sync's Timberlake." Now, it was just "Justin Timberlake," since he was fast becoming a superstar in his own right.

Following the rigorous *Celebrity* tour, which included Sean "P. Diddy" Combs as an opening act, 'N Sync was ready to take a break. This 2002 break was much needed because the individual members of the band were increasingly being presented with broader opportunities. Members were offered acting gigs and feature singing parts. Lance Bass was even invited to be an astronaut!

As of November 2007, 'N Sync has not been back to the recording studio for a fourth album.

Rap heavy-hitters, such as P. Diddy, showed an openness and acceptance of 'N Sync as artists. They were hit makers at a level that could not be ignored.

Bass told Yahoo!'s Launch Radio Networks that the band's break was supposed be a year and a half long. In 2003, Timberlake had confirmed with Launch Radio Networks that the group would do a fourth album eventually. Yet in 2005, he sounded less certain, saying that whether or not 'N Sync ever gets back together, the band will remain close. "Our relationship goes way deeper than records," he said. "Those are my brothers."

Gone Solo

Justin Timberlake released his first solo album, *Justified*, on November 5, 2002. That year, he told Yahoo!'s Launch that a solo album was "something that's kind of been an ongoing thing for me as a kid." The project came about because he simply had a creative spurt and went into the studio. With artists Stevie Wonder and the Eagles as his inspirations, Timberlake cowrote all of the songs on *Justified*. On many of them, he shared writing credit with the Neptunes. Sean "P. Diddy" Combs and Timbaland were among the producers of the album. Janet Jackson sang on one track, "Take Me Now (And She Said)."

Justified was on Billboard's Top R & B/Hip-Hop Albums chart for sixty-eight weeks. It peaked at the number-two slot. Just prior to the album's release, Timberlake performed at the 2002 MTV

Video Music Awards. He premiered the song "Like I Love You." Some critics felt that he copied Michael Jackson a little too much in both his moves and his style, but that criticism did not hurt sales of the album. *Justified* sold more than one million copies in less than a month, according to *Rolling Stone*. Unfortunately, Timberlake broke his foot during that time and had to rest instead of going on tour to support the album.

Around the release of *Justified*, Timberlake was also dealing with his very public breakup with pop star Britney Spears. He made a few comments in the press about the nature of their split. The press then assumed that "Cry Me a River" was about Spears, even going as far as pointing out that the actor playing Timberlake's ex in the video looked a lot like Spears. After Spears released her "Toxic" video, *US* magazine declared

Justin and Britney had their troubles, just like all couples. Their relationship became fodder for the public.

Timberlake Tidbits

- Timberlake has a tattoo on his back of an angel holding a banner. His mother's initials, LRH, are on the banner with the word "Guardian." He told *Rolling Stone* that they have a special relationship: "She's been my best friend since I figured out who I wanted to be."

- Timberlake may have started by singing other people's music, but he's established himself as a talented collaborative and solo songwriter. He has ninety-three credits as a composer with the American Society of Composers, Authors, and Publishers (ASCAP).

- While promoting *Justified*, Timberlake agreed to perform at the "Toronto Rocks" SARS Benefit on July 30, 2003. Other acts included the Rolling Stones, Rush, and AC/DC. Unfortunately, Timberlake was pelted with trash from booing fans during his performance. He still managed to finish his set. He later returned to sing "Miss You" with Mick Jagger of the Rolling Stones. Timberlake joked after the show with reporters about being an unwelcome performer. "It's natural," he said. "If I came to see AC/DC, I wouldn't want to see me either."

- Timberlake loves basketball. In 2003, Turner Sports hired him to be a special correspondent for shows such as *Inside the NBA*. He played in the NBA All-Star Celebrity Games in 2002, 2003, and 2004. He also wrote the theme song for ABC's NBA coverage. In addition, Timberlake hosted a 2007 MTV awards show at the Palm's NBA Hardwood Suite, which happened to be the only hotel suite with an indoor basketball court.

that the two were at war. It was reported that the two were using their art to publicly slam each other.

In January 2003, Timberlake told *Rolling Stone* magazine that the "Cry Me a River" video was not about Britney Spears at all. He revealed that he did call her after the video, however, "because . . . I didn't want things to get misunderstood. She was cool. We're cool." Although the public insisted on believing that the two performers were at war, Timberlake told *Rolling Stone* that he played the "bad guy" in his video, not the female actor.

"Like I Love You" reached number 11 on the Billboard Hot 100 chart and number 53 on the Hot R & B/Hip-Hop Singles and Tracks chart. "Rock Your Body" was another hit for Timberlake. He went on to partner with Christina Aguilera on a U.S. and European tour, which was called Justified/Stripped. Timberlake was nominated for—and won—several awards for his debut album.

According to *People* magazine, this winning streak "justified" Justin Timberlake as a true solo artist. He spoke to one billion television viewers from the MTV Europe Music Awards, saying, "I feel really, really blessed." He was only twenty-two years old, but his solo career was well on its way.

Chapter Four

Tomorrow's Ideas

While topping the music charts, Justin Timberlake had also been going through piles of movie scripts. He actually had acted throughout his career up to that point. He had roles in *Longshot* (2000), *Model Behavior* (2000), and *On the Line* (2001), but they were all minor films.

Timberlake was now ready to do work in feature films. He preferred to act in dramas, rather than comedies and romances. In 2006, he told Yahoo!'s Launch that he "wanted to take [film work] seriously, and I wanted to be taken seriously." Timberlake patterned his acting choices after those of musician-turned-movie star Mark Wahlberg. "He took some time off from the music and took roles where he could show some real chops," Timberlake told Launch. "I guess I'm close to doing the same thing."

Drama

In February 2004, Timberlake was cast for his first major film role. It was in *Edison Force*, a crime drama starring Morgan Freeman, Kevin Spacey, and LL Cool J. *Edison Force* was released in 2006, but it went straight to DVD. Because the film was not in theaters, Timberlake's first attempt at serious acting went unnoticed.

He landed another dramatic role in October of that same year. He had a supporting part in *Alpha Dog*, which featured Sharon Stone and Bruce Willis. The movie was based on a true story about a murder. Released in January 2007, *Alpha Dog* was well received at the highly attended Sundance Film Festival. Timberlake received favorable reviews from film critics for his role.

Timberlake made headway in his role in *Alpha Dog*. He was believable in his portrayal of a person emotionally conflicted over killing a person he liked.

Timberlake was nominated for an MTV Movie Award in 2007 for his breakthrough performance in *Alpha Dog*. He was also nominated for a Teen Choice Award: Breakout Male Performance for *Alpha Dog* and another film, *Black Snake Moan*. *Black Snake Moan* was released in 2007 and starred Samuel L. Jackson and Christina Ricci. Timberlake played the boyfriend of Ricci's character. *Black Snake Moan* was an odd mix of comedy, drama, and romance. It had very mature topics, so it did not reach too many younger viewers.

He acted in another film, the sci-fi drama *Southland Tales*. It was released in 2006 in Europe and in 2007 in the United States. Production on *Southland Tales* began in August 2005. Timberlake played a wounded veteran in the film. Other members of the cast were Sarah Michelle Gellar and Mandy Moore. Despite this abundance of fresh, young talent, film critics did not praise *Southland Tales* for various reasons.

Pure Comedy

In July 2006, Justin Timberlake joined the cast of *Shrek the Third*, which also included Mike Myers and Eddie Murphy. He provided the voice for Artie, the young King Arthur. His real-life girlfriend of four years, Cameron Diaz, was a member of the cast as well.

Timberlake lent his famous voice to the *Shrek* series. He attended world premiers, such as this one in Rome in 2007. The artist was now a globally recognized actor.

Timberlake and Diaz ended their romantic relationship the following spring, just before the film's release.

Returning to Music

In June 2006, Timberlake announced that he was ready to release his second solo album, which he had been working on since December 2005, according to *Rolling Stone* magazine. He took a leisurely approach to creating it. He told *Rolling Stone* that his influences were varied, including Coldplay, the Killers, and Prince. David Bowie and David Byrne were his inspirations for the album's first single, "SexyBack." The album was called *FutureSex/LoveSounds* (*FS/LS*).

The sound of the new album signaled yet another change for Timberlake and the music industry. The MTV Artist of the Week spotlight asserted that *FS/LS* would provide "the musical roadmap for pop in the next year." Timberlake and his team had created tomorrow's music today, said reviewers. Producers of the album included Timberlake, Timbaland, Danja (Nate Hills), and Rick Rubin. Danja has partnered with Timbaland for radio-friendly artists such as Katharine McPhee. Rubin produced the Red Hot Chili Peppers and LL Cool J. Featured vocalists on *FS/LS* included Timbaland and T. I.

Timberlake released "SexyBack" on September 7, 2006. *FS/LS* came out five days later, on September 12, 2006. The album debuted on Billboard's Top 200 in the number-one spot. It also shot to the top of Billboard's Top Digital Albums and Top Internet Albums charts. In addition, it was number 1 on

The success of *FutureSex/LoveSounds* firmly placed Justin Timberlake in the music industry as a strong, talented solo artist. Timberlake created hits while also experimenting with hip-hop to produce deeper pop.

Music, Mending, and Munching

Despite his taking on various acting projects, Timberlake still found time to lend his voice to the songs of other artists. He collaborated with the Black Eyed Peas on their "Where Is the Love?" and "My Style." Timberlake's other collaborations include Timbaland's "Give It to Me," which featured Nelly Furtado, as well as Furtado's own song "Crowd Control." He also recorded "Signs" for Snoop Dogg. While working on Snoop's "Signs," Timberlake made a startling discovery. Something was affecting his singing.

At twenty-four years old, Timberlake discovered that he had nodules, or growths, on his vocal chords. Overstretching his vocal cords caused the nodules to form. Although the growths were benign, or harmless, they still needed to be removed. On May 5, 2005, Timberlake had surgery to remove the growths at Cedars Sinai Hospital in Los Angeles. He would need to rest his voice for at least three months. During this time, his mind turned to business ideas, such as his own record label and restaurants.

Timberlake first entered the restaurant business back in 2003. He co-owned Chi Club in California, with Art and Allan Davis. The club is now closed. In February 2006, however, he opened the Southern-Italian cuisine restaurant Destino in New York with his business partner, Eytan Sugarman. Timberlake and Eytan opened another New York restaurant in March 2007. Called Southern Hospitality, the restaurant serves up southern home-style dishes.

the Top R&B/Hip-Hop Albums chart. *FS/LS*'s next single was "My Love"; it was released in October 2006. It was followed by "What Goes Around…/…Comes Around" in February 2007. Ultimately, the album would produce four number-one singles.

The FutureSex/LoveSounds Tour started in January 2007. In addition to singing and doing fancy footwork, Timberlake played guitar, keyboards, and piano on this tour. Guests included young R & B stars Pink and Rihanna. According to the Perth *Sunday Times*, Timberlake warmed up the entire stadium by playing Nine Inch Nails' "Closer." He sent concert goers home listening to the Verve's "Bittersweet Symphony."

Tomorrow's Projects: New Clothes, New Discs

Despite the amazing success of his second solo album, Timberlake is not done innovating. With his longtime friend and assistant, Trace Ayala, he introduced a new spring clothing line in October 2006. Ayala and Timberlake named the line William Rast, after their grandfathers. The clothing line offers a range of items for both men and women and is sold at higher-end stores such as Nordstrom.

In May 2007, Timberlake launched his own record label, Tennman Records, in partnership with Universal Music Group's

Interscope Geffen A & M. His label is based in Los Angeles, California, and he is already developing talent. "I cannot wait to introduce the world to my new discoveries," Timberlake told the Associated Press.

In addition to discovering and developing talent, Timberlake loaned his vocal, producing, writing, and musical skills to fellow artists. He worked with pop superstar Madonna. As of August 2007, Timberlake, Timbaland, and Madonna had already produced six tracks for her upcoming album, according to the Perth *Sunday Times*. Working with Madonna has been very exciting for Timberlake. "There are definitely moments when I think, 'Wow, I'm singing with Madonna,'" he said.

He has proved time and again that an artist isn't limited to being a triple threat. An artist should continue to be innovative, never limiting himself or herself to just a few talents. Timberlake actively seeks to develop the skills he has—and to obtain those that he doesn't yet have. At the core of this incredibly talented, driven artist is something quite simple: a fan. Timberlake told the Perth *Sunday Times*, "At the end of the day, I'm just a music fan."

Timeline

1992 Timberlake appears on *Star Search* as Justin Timberlake Randall.

1993 He joins *The All New Mickey Mouse Club*.

1995 *The All New Mickey Mouse Club* ends; Timberlake links up with JC Chasez to form 'N Sync.

1998 RCA Records releases **NSYNC* in the United States.

1999 Timberlake and the other members of 'N Sync have legal issues with Ron Pearlman.

2000 'N Sync releases *No Strings Attached*; Timberlake lands acting roles in *Model Behavior* and *Longshot*.

2001 *Celebrity* is released, and Timberlake tours behind it into 2002; he acts in *On the Line*.

2002 Timberlake records his first solo album, *Justified*.

2003 Timberlake joins Christina Aguilera on a joint Justified/Stripped tour.

2006 He hosts the European MTV Music Awards; appears on *Saturday Night Live*; launches clothing line.

2007 *Shrek the Third* is released; Timberlake launches Tennman Records; receives an Emmy for a *Saturday Night Live* sketch with comedian Andy Samberg.

2008 Timberlake hosts the Las Vegas PGA Tour.

Discography

Albums with 'N Sync

1998 *NSYNC
1998 *Home for Christmas* (in Europe, *The Winter Album*)
2000 *No Strings Attached*
2001 *Celebrity*
2005 *Greatest Hits*

Albums as Solo Artist

2002 *Justified*
2006 *FutureSex/LoveSounds*

Singles

2002 "Like I Love You," "Cry Me a River"
2003 "Rock Your Body," "Senorita," "I'm Lovin' It"
2006 "SexyBack," "My Love"
2007 "What Goes Around . . . Comes Around," "Summer Love," "LoveStoned," "Until the End of Time"

Collaborations

2002 "Work It" (Nelly)
2003 "Where Is the Love?" (Black Eyed Peas)
2005 "Signs" (Snoop Dogg)
2007 "Give It to Me" (Nelly Furtado/Timbaland), "Ayo Technology" (50 Cent/ Timbaland), "Falling Down" (Duran Duran), "Nite Runner" (Duran Duran/ Timbaland), "The Only Promise That Remains" (Reba McEntire)

Glossary

capitalize To profit from or take advantage of something.

collaborative Working with others.

genre An artistic category that has a particular format, style, or subject matter.

idolize To show great admiration or loyalty to someone.

medley Combination of two or more songs.

melodies An arrangement of notes that are either played or sung.

meteoric With great speed or brilliance.

Motown A star-making music company based out of Detroit, Michigan. It produced dozens of pop, soul, and gospel hits in the 1960s and 1970s.

paparazzi People who aggressively photograph celebrities.

producer A person who organizes and supervises the making of a song or entire album.

R & B (rhythm and blues) A style of music originally developed by African Americans that blends blues and jazz.

rock and roll A genre of music that combines elements of blues, jazz, country, and western music.

royalty A percentage of a profit from a creative endeavor.

For More Information

Canadian Country Music
    Association
626 King Street West, Suite 203
Toronto, ON M5V 1M7
Canada
(416) 947-1331
E-mail: country@ccma.org
Web site: http://www.cirpa.ca
This is a non-profit professional
    trade organization whose
    purpose is to protect the
    heritage of, advocate the
    development of, and enact
    laws favorable to Canadian
    country music.

Zomba Label Group
137–139 West 25th Street
New York, NY 10001
(212) 727-0016

Web site: http://www.
    zombalabelgroup.com
This is the parent company of
    Jive Records. It's also a part
    of Sony BMG Entertainment.
    You can learn about Justin
    Timberlake and other
    bands from its Web site.

Web Sites

Due to the changing nature of
Internet links, Rosen Publishing
has developed an online list of
Web sites related to the subject
of this book. This site is
updated regularly. Please use
this link to access the list:

http://www.rosenlinks.com/
    cmtm/juti

For Further Reading

Hannah, Jonny. *Hot Jazz Special*. Cambridge, MA: Candlewick Press, 2005.

Hatch, Thomas, and Timothy V. Rasinski. *History of Hip-Hop: The Roots of Rap*. Mankato, MN: Coughlan Publishing, 2005.

Hoffman, Frank, and Richard Carlin. *Rhythm and Blues, Rap, and Hip-Hop*. New York, NY: Facts On File, 2005.

Lucent Books. *Justin Timberlake*. Farmington Mills, MI: Gale Group, 2008.

Marcovitz, Hal. *Justin Timberlake*. Broomall, PA: Mason Crest Publishing, 2007.

Raso, Anne, and Kimberly Walsh. *Backstage Pass: Just Justin*. New York, NY: Scholastic, 2000.

Stalling Huntington, Carla. *Hip-Hop Dance: Meanings and Messages*. Jefferson, NC: McFarland & Company, 2007.

Tracy, Kathy. *Justin Timberlake*. Hockessin, DE: Mitchell Lane Publishers, 2007.

Bibliography

Bass, Lance, and Marc Eliot. *Out of Sync*. New York, NY: Simon & Schuster, 2007.

Gregory, Andy. *International Who's Who in Popular Music 2002*. New York, NY: Routledge Publishing, 2002.

Hedegaard, Erik. "The Bachelor." *Rolling Stone*, January 23, 2003. Retrieved October 10, 2007 (http://www.rollingstone.com/news/coverstory/timberlake_the_bachelor/page/2).

Mehr, Bob. "Embrace the Blues (and Punk and Hip-Hop) with Spin's Guide to Memphis." Spin.com, December 4, 2007. Retrieved December 7, 2007 (http://www.spin.com/features/magazine/2007/12/0712_memphis_rock_city).

Smith, Sean. *Justin: The Unauthorized Biography*. New York, NY: Simon & Schuster, 2005.

Index

About the Author

Holly Cefrey is an award-winning children's book author. After moving to New York from Nebraska, she attended classes at the School for Film and Television. At the school, Cefrey studied facets of the entertainment industry, and as a result, became interested in the behind-the-scenes side of the industry. She came to work at dynamic casting agencies such as Stark Naked Productions and Alycia Aumuller Casting. She has supported casting projects for voice-over/radio, theater, music videos, television, and film.

Photo Credits

Designer: Gene Mollica; **Editor:** Nicholas Croce; **Photo Researcher:** Amy Feinberg